MW01172010

Elementary School

The History and Activities of the

FRONTIER

Lisa Klobuchar

Heinemann Library
Chicago, Illinois

Customer Service 888-454-2279
Visit our website at www.heinemannraintree.com

Designed by Richard Parker and Tinstar Design Ltd (www.tinstar.co.uk)
Printed and bound in China by WKT Company Limited

10 09 08 07 06
10 9 8 7 6 5 4 3 2 1

Library of Congress Cataloging-in-Publication Data

Klobuchar, Lisa.

The history and activities of the frontier / Lisa Klobuchar.
    p. cm. -- (Hands-on American history)
 Includes bibliographical references and index.
 ISBN 1-4034-6056-6 -- ISBN 1-4034-6063-9 (pbk.)
 1. Frontier and pioneer life--United States--Study and teaching--Activity programs--Juvenile literature. 2. United States--Social life and customs--Study and teaching--Activity programs--Juvenile literature. I. Title. II. Series.
 E179.5.K546 2004
 973--dc22

                            2004003884

Acknowledgments
The author and publishers are grateful to the following for permission to reproduce copyright material: Bridgeman Art Library p. 10 (New York Historical Society, New York, USA); Britstock pp. 18; Corbis pp. 13 (Museum of the City of New York), 6 (Connie Ricca), 26; Getty Images p. 5 (Hulton Archive); Harcourt Education pp. 17, 21, 25, 29 (Janet Moran); Kentucky Library & Museum p. 16; Mary Evans Picture Library p. 11; Minnesota Historical Society Library p. 14; North Wind Picture Archive pp. 8, 9, 12, 15; Photographers Direct p. 22 (Michael P. Gadomski).

Cover photographs by Bridgeman Art Library/New York Historical Society and Mary Evans Picture Library

Contents

Some words are shown in bold, **like this**. You can find out what they mean by looking in the glossary.

Chapter 1: Pioneer Spirit

Settling east of the Mississippi

From the late 1700s to the 1830s, the only well-established cities and towns in the United States were in the far eastern regions. At that time, the country was made up of only 24 states. Nearly all the land west of the Appalachian Mountains was wild **frontier**. The chance for cheap land and new opportunities in these unclaimed lands drew many **pioneers** to the west.

Pioneers had to be daring, imaginative, and independent. Leaving everything that was familiar and starting fresh in a wild land was full of risks. Some early pioneers were Americans, but many were **immigrants** from Europe. Single men or entire families made the trip. They settled in Kentucky, Tennessee, Ohio, Indiana, Illinois, and other regions as far west as the Mississippi Valley.

Early pioneers made their way to the Northwest Territory through thick forests and climbed the Appalachian Mountains with their belongings strapped to a couple of pack horses. Later, with all the belongings they could load

TIME LINE

1845	1848	1853	1862
Texas becomes part of United States.	Treaty of Guadalupe Hidalgo ends Mexican War. United States gains all of Mexico's territory in what is now called the Southwest.	Gadsden Purchase adds the southern parts of what are now Arizona and New Mexico to United States.	Homestead Act gives 160 acres (65 hectares) of land free to anyone who had lived on the land and improved it for five years.

4

into their wagons, they traveled along the National Road. This road was begun in 1811 and eventually stretched from western Pennsylvania all the way to Illinois. Others boarded flatboats and journeyed along the Ohio River. Still others headed for the wild country known as the Old Southwest.

The soil in the east was **fertile**, rain was plentiful, and the woods, marshes, and meadows were full of deer, bears, rabbits, wild turkey, ducks, geese, and many other animals to hunt. Even so, trees had to be cleared and rocks removed to prepare the ground for farming. Homes and barns had to be built. Crops had to be planted and harvested. Life was challenging for the pioneers.

This 19th Century painting shows a typical wagon train crossing the plains.

West of the Mississippi

Pioneers did not begin to settle west of the Mississippi River until after 1840. However, the first steps of this **migration** were taken in the early 1800s.

In 1803 President Thomas Jefferson bought a large area of land from the French. The land deal, called the Louisiana Purchase, added to the United States all the territory from Canada in the north to the Gulf of Mexico, and from the Mississippi Valley in the east to the Rocky Mountains in the west. In 1853 the size of the country doubled again, as the United States took over lands west of the Rockies, all the way to the Pacific Ocean. By 1853 the country's borders looked much as they do today.

Pioneers settled the far western areas of the country first. Beginning about 1840, large numbers of Americans and settlers from other countries began pouring into the lands

Thomas Jefferson signing the Louisiana Purchase.

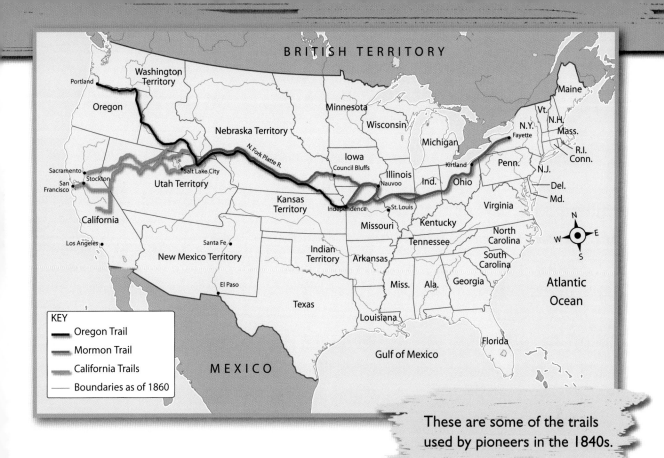

BRITISH TERRITORY

KEY
— Oregon Trail
— Mormon Trail
— California Trails
— Boundaries as of 1860

These are some of the trails used by pioneers in the 1840s.

west of the Mississippi River. They traveled more than 2,000 miles (3,219 kilometers) along the Oregon, California, and Mormon trails. Many had heard reports of attractive land regions, fertile farmlands, and mild climates and wanted to start farms there. Others went simply in search of the chance to make a fresh start in a new land. After gold was discovered in California in 1849, many others came with the hope of getting rich. In all, more than 500,000 settlers—including as many as 250,000 children—made the difficult and exhausting trip over wilderness trails in wagons.

It was only after 1860 that settlers started claiming land in the Great Plains region in the middle of the country. In 1862 the Homestead Act gave 160 acres (65 hectares) of land free to anyone who had lived on the land and improved it for five years. This encouraged many farmers to settle on the Great Plains.

Chapter 2: Life in New Lands

Usually the first order of business for **pioneer** families was to build a place to live. In the heavily forested wilderness of the Old Southwest, the Northwest Territory, and the Far West, this usually meant building a log cabin. Log cabins were made with rough logs notched and fitted together.

On the Great Plains, it was harder to find enough wood to build log cabins. Tall grasses covered most of the land. So, many Great Plains pioneers built sod houses. Sod houses were built out of the tightly packed roots of grasses and the soil that clung to it. Sometimes they built their homes partially underground in the side of a small hill. This kept the houses cooler in the summer and warmer in the winter.

Furnishing a home

Pioneer families often had to make their own furniture and supplies when they set up their homes. A large log cut in half could serve as a table, with legs made of four smaller branches. Three-legged stools were made in a similar way. Many pioneers whittled, or carved, cups and bowls from wood.

Notice how alone this log cabin is in the woods.

8

Frontier women did all their cooking over the open fire in the fireplace. They would hang a large cast iron pot over the flames to cook stews and soups. They grilled on a gridiron and fried in a long-handled skillet. They baked food in a bake kettle, which was a skillet raised on three short legs and topped with a snug-fitting lid.

Skilled craftspeople supplied the pioneers with many tools and furnishings. At their fiery furnaces, blacksmiths hammered heavy items from iron, such as horseshoes and ax blades. Cabinetmakers made cabinets and other wooden furniture. Coopers had the important job of making barrels used to store everything from apple cider to cornmeal. Tanners made leather from animal hides. Tinsmiths or tinkers, made household items from tin plate. Tin plate is a sheet of steel coated with a very thin layer of tin, a type of soft metal.

The **pioneers** made many household items by themselves. One reason for doing this was to save money. They also made their own items because in many areas there were no skilled craftspeople selling what the pioneers needed.

Pioneer families could sometimes buy pottery, but sometimes they made their own. To make their own pottery, pioneer families dug clay from the ground, mixed it with water, and formed it into various types of vessels. Then they put the vessels into an open fire. After hours and hours of baking, the clay hardened into a strong material called earthenware.

Clothing

When it came to clothing, pioneers often had to make everything themselves. They even had to raise their own sheep for wool and grow their own plants, such as cotton and flax, for fibers.

This pitcher was made in 1798.

10

Flax fibers were used to make linen cloth. Preparing the flax fibers for spinning into thread was a long process. First, pioneers separated the usable fibers from the flax stalks by pounding them in a machine called a flax break. Then they had to slash and comb the fibers to remove every bit of stalk.

Often by the light of the fireplace, a pioneer woman used a spinning wheel to spin flax fibers into yarn. She turned the wheel by pumping with a foot pedal called a treadle. The spinning wheel twisted the raw linen fibers into yarn.

Pioneer families also spun their own wool yarn. After sheep were sheared, or shaved, mats and burrs had to be removed from the raw wool through a process called carding. Pioneers carded wool by combing it between two paddles covered with short metal teeth.

Once there was enough yarn, it could be used it to weave cloth. The cloth then was used to make clothes and household items such as napkins and placemats.

Blacksmiths were an important part of the pioneer community.

Pioneer food

Corn became one of the most important foods for **pioneers**. Corn was easy to grow in the newly cleared plots of land. This corn provided pioneers with a nutritious grain that could be stored easily year round and used in many ways. They ground the dried kernels into cornmeal. They used cornmeal to make cornbread, hoecake, johnnycake, corn pone, and cornmeal mush. They softened whole, dried kernels and then boiled them to make hominy. Hominy was served with pork gravy in a filling dish called hog and hominy. In the South, hominy was ground up and cooked into a food called grits.

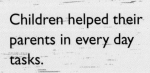

Children helped their parents in every day tasks.

Fresh meat was a treat in the pioneer's diet.

When their fields were ready, new pioneers began growing squash, potatoes, pumpkins, beans, and turnips. Green vegetables were not a big part of the pioneer diet. Neither were white sugar, coffee, or tea. Most families could not afford to buy these treats, and they were used only on special occasions. For sweetening, they used honey, maple syrup, and molasses.

Meat made up the other main part of the pioneers' diet. Pioneer families raised chickens, sheep, pigs, and cattle. They caught fish in the lakes and streams. They also hunted forest and wetland animals such as duck, turkey, deer, squirrel, rabbit, opossum, and bear.

Chapter 3: Pioneers at Play

Pioneers expected to do most of their work on their own, but they also knew that they could get help from their neighbors when they needed it. They often got together to do tasks as a group. Group tasks included clearing land, building houses, and various harvest tasks. These get-togethers, often called bees, usually combined work with play and socializing. They gave people a chance to share news and get to know new neighbors. Men, women, and children all participated in the bees with different tasks.

Children's playtime

Pioneer life was hard work, and adults expected their children to help out as soon as they were old enough. Pioneer children helped collect firewood and pick wild berries, mushrooms, and herbs. Girls helped their mothers with household chores while boys hunted and worked in the fields with their fathers. But they still found time for fun.

Building a barn was an important community event. This photograph is from a barn raising in Minnesota.

Pioneer children had little time for play.

Pioneer kids played hide and seek, hopscotch, marbles, and pick-up-sticks. They pulled each other around in wagons and went sledding in the winter. Unlike today's toys, pioneer toys were simple. Many of them were homemade, either by the parents or by the children themselves. Whistles carved from willow branches, bow-and-arrow sets, and fishing poles provided entertainment for boys. Girls played with homemade dolls and jump ropes.

Buzz saws, dolls, whirligigs, jack-in-the-boxes, and jumping jacks were some of the toys popular in pioneer days. Jumping jacks were flat puppets whose arms and legs moved when you pulled a string.

By doing the hands-on activities and crafts in this chapter, you'll get a feel for what life was like for people who lived and worked on the **frontier** in the 1800s.

Recipe: Make Kentucky Burgoo

This hearty meat-and-vegetable stew was a favorite at **pioneer** celebrations in Kentucky and surrounding areas. No one is exactly sure how the recipe developed. Burgoo would include several different kinds of meats, including lamb, pork, opossum, and squirrel.

Making a large batch of burgoo was a community event.

WARNING

Always make sure an adult is present when using a hot stove.

Make sure to read all the directions before starting the recipe.

INGREDIENTS

- 1 tablespoon of vegetable oil
- 10 ounces (570 grams) of boneless, skinless chicken, cut into large chunks
- 10 ounces (570 grams) of boneless pork meat, cut into large chunks
- half an onion, diced
- 1 clove of garlic, crushed
- 2 tablespoons flour
- 2 14.5-ounce (410-gram) cans of chicken or beef broth
- 1 14.5-ounce (410-gram) can of whole tomatoes, cut up
- 1 cup (230 grams) sliced carrots
- 2 cups (450 grams) cubed potatoes
- 1 cup (230 grams) frozen lima beans
- 1 cup (230 grams) frozen sliced okra
- 1 cup (230 grams) frozen corn

1. Heat the oil in a large stew pot over medium heat. Add the pork and chicken and stir until they are browned. Transfer the meat to a bowl.

2. Add the onion and garlic to the pot and fry until soft.

3. Sprinkle the flour over the onion and garlic and stir until the onion and garlic are well coated.

4. Add the broth to the pot slowly while stirring. Stir until the mixture thickens.

5. Add the tomatoes and the meat and bring to a boil. Lower the heat, cover the pot, and simmer until all the meat is tender. This will take about 1 1/2 hours.

6. Add the carrots and potatoes. Simmer for 10 minutes.

7. Add the lima beans, okra, and corn. Simmer until everything is tender (about 20 minutes).

Craft: Weave a Placemat

Most of the cloth woven by **pioneer** women was linsey-woolsey, a mixture of linen and wool yarn. Linsey-woolsey was made on a large loom called a barn frame loom. The loom had a four-sided frame with a bench to sit on. The loom itself was inside this frame. They made brownish-yellow, black, and blue dyes for linsey-woolsey out of different kinds of tree bark.

This modern woman is demonstrating how pioneer women carded the wool before weaving.

WORDS TO KNOW

loom structure on which something can be woven

warp yarn that lies lengthwise in weaving

weave to move yarn in an over-under-over-under pattern to make cloth

weft yarn that lies crossways in weaving.

1. Holding the ball of string or yarn, tape one end to the corner of a cake pan. The cake pan will be used as a loom. Pull the string across the pan to the opposite side and tape it to the edge of the pan.

2. Unwind more string and pull it back across the pan to the first side. Tape it down to the edge of the box, about 1/4 inch (2/3 centimeters) from where you started. Keep running the string back and forth across the box, taping it at each side. Each length of string should be about 1/4 inch (2/3 centimeters) apart. These strings that lie lengthwise are known as the warp. (See Picture A)

SUPPLIES

- small cake pan or shallow box
- tape
- ball of string or yarn
- yarn in different colors, each piece about 10 feet (3 meters) long.
- scissors
- paper clip or yarn needle (optional)
- fork or comb (optional)

A

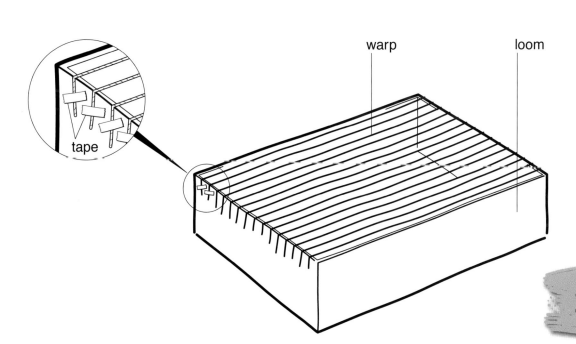

tape

warp   loom

3. Cut a piece of yarn about 10 feet (3 meters) long. This will be your weft thread. Weft thread is thread that lies crosswise. You can tie the yarn to a paper clip, use a yarn needle, or simply use your finger.

4. Starting on one side, tie your weft thread to one end of your warp thread. Pass the yarn over the first warp thread, and under the next one. Continue this over-and-under pattern until you reach the other side. (See Picture B)

5. When you reach the other side, pull the thread through the warp until the end of the thread just hangs over the edge.

6. Now you are ready to start weaving in the opposite direction. You always weave the opposite way from the row before. If you ended the last row by going under the warp, now you will start by going over. Continue the over-under-over pattern until you reach the opposite side. (See Picture C)

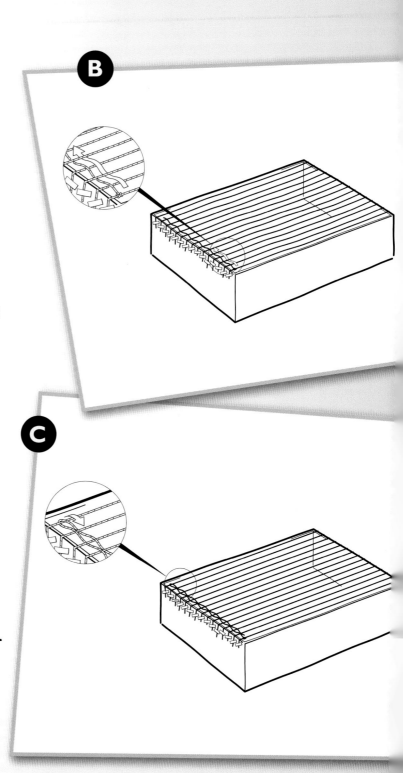

B

C

7. Use a fork, comb, or your fingers to nudge the weft thread tightly against the previous row.

8. If you reach the end of your yarn, or you want to change colors, tie the end to the warp thread, then tie on the new yarn. (See Picture D)

9. When you finish weaving your yarn over the entire warp, tie your weft thread to the last warp thread.

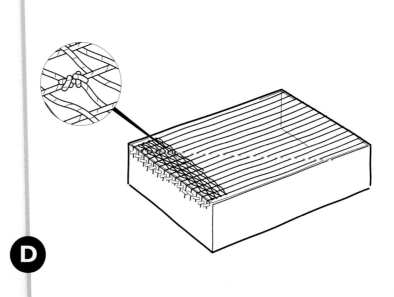

D

10. Peel the tape off the box and take your new placemat off the loom. *Would you rather use a store bought placemat or one you made yourself? Why?*

Craft: Make a Tin Lantern

Tinsmiths on the **frontier** used strong scissors, rounded hammers, and awls to cut, shape, and decorate tin objects. They used solder, or melted metal, to join pieces of tin together. Tin lanterns were useful because they could protect a burning candle from wind, while allowing light to shine through. The light shining through the pattern punched in the tin made a pleasing sight on a dark night.

This tinware is from the 1800s.

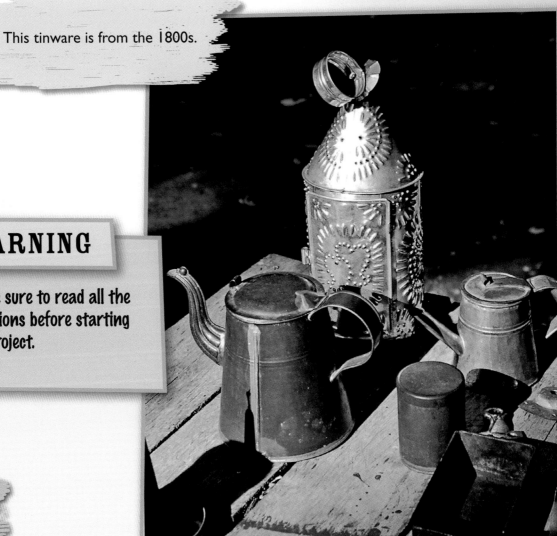

SUPPLIES

- tooling foil or foil cookie sheet, about 10 inches (25 centimeters) by 15 inches (38 centimeters)
- ruler
- scissors
- pointed metal skewer, awl, or leather punch
- flathead screwdriver
- heavy cardboard
- brass paper fasteners
- 2-inch (5-centimeter) round cardboard roll (A wrapping paper roll is a good size, or you can use a toilet paper or paper towel roll.)

1. Cut a piece of foil 4 inches (10 centimeters) by 9 inches (23 centimeters).

2. Fold over 1/4 inch (6 millimeters) on the long sides.

3. There is an example of a pattern for a **pioneer** lantern on this page (See Picture A). Copy this pattern or create your own pattern. Make sure to cut your pattern so it is the same size as your foil.

A

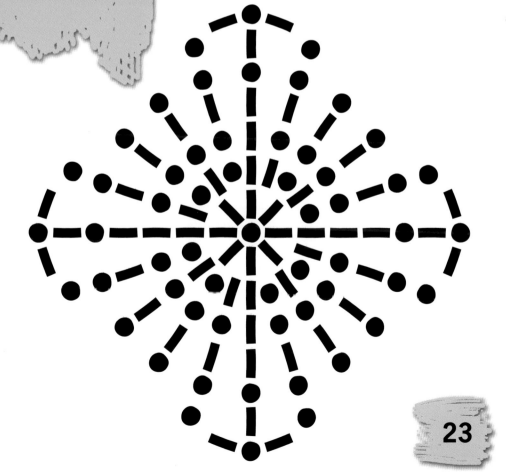

4. Place the foil onto a piece of heavy cardboard with the folded pieces facing down. Center your pattern drawing on the foil and tape it down.

5. Use the skewer to punch out round holes. Use the screwdriver to punch out slits. *What else can you use to create shapes in the foil?*

6. Wrap the foil around the cardboard roll with the two plain, short ends of the foil overlapping (See Picture B).

7. Punch a hole through both layers of foil near the top and bottom. Attach the two sides together with the paper fasteners (See Picture C).

8. Slide the foil tube off of the cardboard tube.

9. Ask an adult to help you slip the lantern over a small candle in a glass holder to complete your tin lantern.

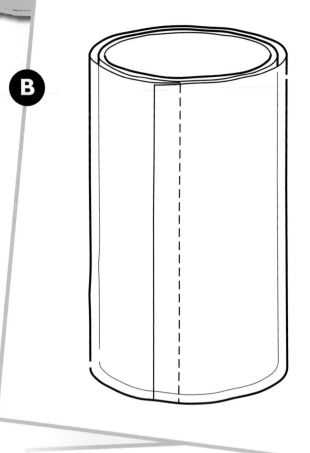

B

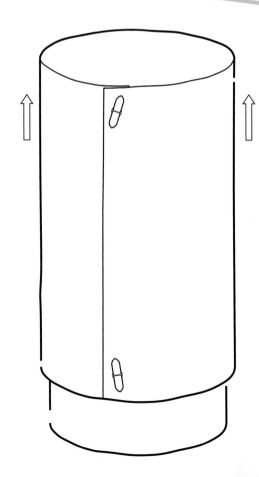

C

Craft: Make a Jacob's Ladder

The Jacob's ladder was a favorite **frontier** toy. It gets its name from a story in the Bible in which a man named Jacob has a vision of a ladder stretching toward heaven.

Wooden toys were popular on the frontier.

1. Have an adult cut six squares of wood, each about 3 inches by 3 inches (8 centimeters by 8 centimeters).

2. Cut 15 pieces of ribbon, each 7 inches (18 centimeters) long.

3. Start with two pieces of wood. Glue the ends of the ribbon pieces to the wood squares as shown. Only glue the ends of the ribbon. You will glue an end down, wrap it around to the other side of the wood, and then glue it to the next piece of wood (See Pictures A and B)

SUPPLIES

- wood slats or balsawood panels (available at craft or hobby stores)
- ruler
- wood saw or utility knife for balsawood
- 3/8- inch ribbon
- scissors
- fabric adhesive (or hot glue with adult supervision)

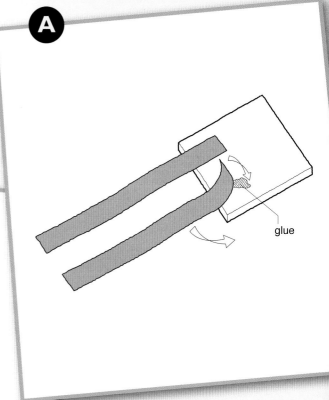

A

glue

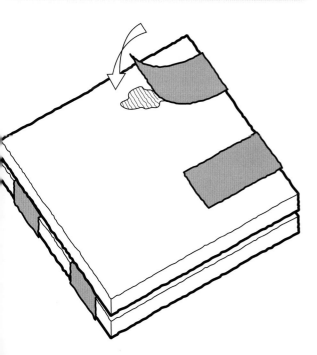

B

4. Add another piece of wood to the first two. Use the same method with the ribbon that you used in step 3.

5. Continue adding wood until you have six pieces connected. Set the squares aside until the adhesive or hot glue dries completely.

6. Take the chain of squares and place it ribbon side down on a table. Now you will add ribbons to the other side. At one end of the squares, glue the end of a ribbon down. Then slide the other end of the ribbon between the first and second squares, along the bottom, and back up between the second and third squares. Glue the end down to the second square. (See Picture C)

7. Just like in step 6, glue another ribbon to the third square, slide it between the third and fourth squares, run it across the bottom of the fourth square, and back up between the fourth and fifth squares. Glue the end down on the fifth square.

8. Repeat these steps until you have connected all of the squares. Let the glue dry.

9. You can trim the extra ends of the ribbons, but make sure you don't trim the middle of the ribbon.

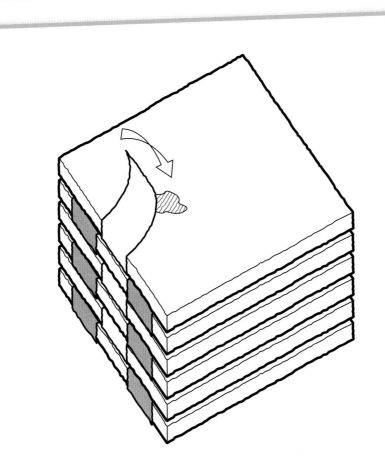

C

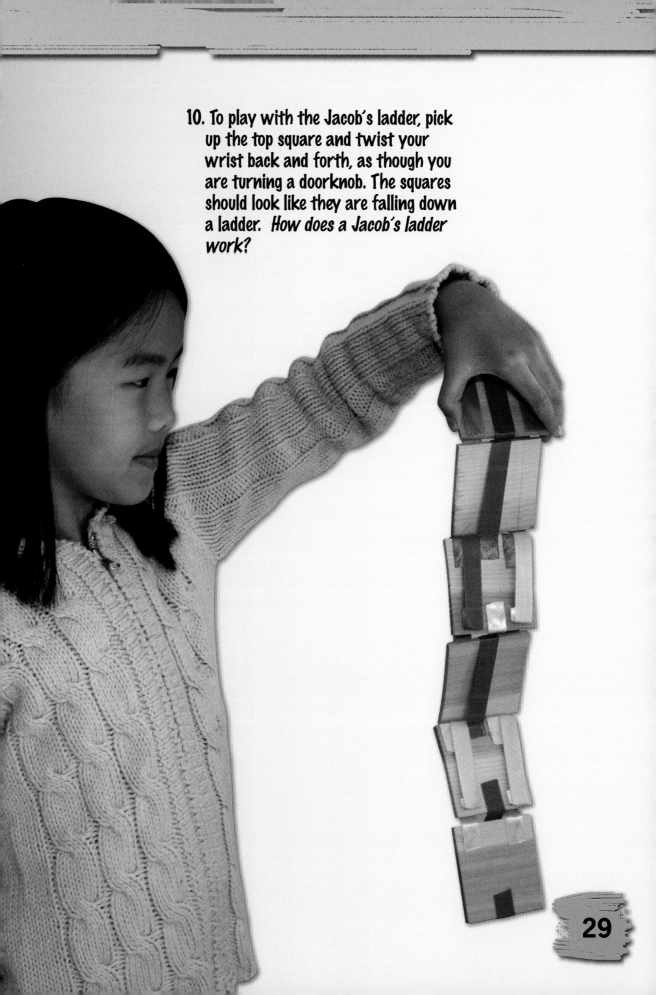

10. To play with the Jacob's ladder, pick up the top square and twist your wrist back and forth, as though you are turning a doorknob. The squares should look like they are falling down a ladder. *How does a Jacob's ladder work?*

29

Glossary

fertile land that is good for growing crops

frontier unsettled land, especially the land on the edge of a settled area

immigrant someone who is born in one country and moves to another

migration movement from one area to another

pioneer person who starts something new

More Books to Read

Isaacs, Sally Senzell. *The Great Land Rush*. Chicago: Heinemann, 2004.

Kalman, Bobbie and Lynda Hale. *Pioneer Recipes*. New York: Crabtree Publishing, 2004.

A Note to Teachers

The instructions for these projects are designed to allow students to work as independently as possible. However, it is always a good idea to make a prototype before assigning any project, so that students can see how their own work will look when completed. Prior to introducing these projects, teachers should collect and prepare the materials and be ready for any modifications that may be necessary. Participating in the project-making process will help teachers understand the directions and be ready to assist students with difficult steps. Teachers might also choose to adapt or modify the lessons to better suit the needs of an individual student or class. No one knows what levels of achievement students will reach better than their teacher.

While it is preferable for students to work as independently as possible, there is some flexibility in regards to project materials and tools. They can vary according to what is available. For instance, while standard white glue may be most familiar to students, there might be times when a teacher will choose to speed up a project by using a hot glue gun to fasten materials for students. Likewise, while a project may call for leather cord, it is feasible in most instances to substitute vinyl cord or even yarn or rope. Acrylic paint may be recommended because it adheres better to a material like felt or plastic, but other types of paint would be useable as well. Circles can be drawn with a compass, or simply by tracing a cup, roll of tape, or other circular object. Obviously, allowing students a broad spectrum of creativity and opportunities to problem-solve within the parameters of a given project will encourage their critical thinking skills most fully.

Each project contains an italicized question somewhere in the directions. These questions are meant to be thought-provoking and promote discussion while students work on the project.

Index